M000252256

Playing Volleyball

An ARM CHAIR GUIDE

Full of 100 Tips to Getting Better at Volleyball

Arm Chair Guides

Playing Volleyball:
An Arm Chair Guide Full of 100 Tips to Getting Better at Volleyball

Published by
Arm Chair Guides

Printed in the United States of America

All rights reserved © 2011 Arm Chair Guides

The editorial arrangement, analysis, and professional commentary are subject to this copyright notice. No portion of this book may be copied, retransmitted, reposted, duplicated, or otherwise used without the express written approval of the author, except by reviewers who may quote brief excerpts in connection with a review. United States laws and regulations are public domain and not subject to copyright. Any unauthorized copying, reproduction, translation, or distribution of any part of this material without permission by the author is prohibited and against the law. Disclaimer and Terms of Use: No information contained in this book should be considered as financial, tax, or legal advice. Your reliance upon information and content obtained by you at or through this publication is solely at your own risk.

The publisher and author assumes no liability or responsibility for damage or injury to you, other persons, or property arising from any use of any product, information, idea, or instruction contained in the content or services provided to you through this book. Reliance upon information contained in this material is solely at the reader's own risk. The author has no financial interest in and receives no compensation from manufacturers of products or websites mentioned in this book.

ISBN-13: 978-0615502069
ISBN-10: 0615502067

Visit the Arm Chair Guides site at:
www.ArmChairGuides.com/PlayingVolleyball

Overview

Enjoyed by people of all ages, volleyball does not require any costly equipment and is fairly easy to learn.

According to the International Volleyball Federation (FIVB), the international body that governs the sport, 1 in 6 people throughout the world either enjoys playing or watching the game.

Whether played indoors or out (such as beach volleyball), it can be played just about anywhere. And although the outdoor variety doesn't require as many players, the rules for both types are virtually identical.

No matter if you intend on playing competitive volleyball or simply want to set up a net at the park, keep reading, and you'll get a handle on the basics of this fun, exciting sport.

Always remember that volleyball is just a game.

There is definitely a problem if you are playing the sport for money or gambling for possessions. The goal is to keep it fun.

A little healthy competition is great as long as someone doesn't end up in tears. Be conscious of other peoples' feelings and be sure you don't prize winning above all else.

Communication is one of the major aspects of the game.

If you are on a team with three or more players, this is especially important. Good communication prevents one team member from overexerting him or herself while the rest of the players run around like chickens with their heads cut off trying to hit the ball.

Use common phrases like "me", "mine" or "got it" for they let your teammates know where you are and that you know your role – as they should.

It's vital that you improve upon the fundamentals of the game.

The first thing you should learn about volleyball will always be the most important: how to bump the ball. This maneuver isn't as forceful as a strike nor is it as graceful as setting the ball, but it's used more frequently. Bumping allows you to control the ball on your side of the court. Good height and good speed are important, for those allow the setter to position him or herself close to the net and drill the ball onto the opponent's side.

Check your shoes.

Leg, ankle and back injuries can result from jumping. Always check that your shoes are tied tightly. Rolled or sprained ankles are often caused by untied shoes. Good, lightweight shoes also absorb shock and provide ankle and arch support.

You can also use tape around your joints to prevent injuries. Don't be afraid to tape up ankles, knees or even your back, for it adds support. Always be safe now rather than sorry later.

Stretch.

When sprinting, you can injure an ankle or pull your groin. Tape and tight shoes help prevent ankle injuries. Stretching helps to prevent groin pulls. At least 5 to 10 minutes of stretching before playing any sport is imperative. It loosens the muscles and prepares the body for whatever activity you are engaged in.

Wear kneepads.

You can get banged up pretty easily in a gym when diving. You can't do much about the slight bruising that will happen. It'll show if you play hard. Wearing kneepads can do a lot to prevent skin burns. For indoor volleyball, kneepads are a must. No matter the surface, they work very well to prevent burns from diving and sliding.

Volleyball is a sport. If you take the proper precautions, you can avoid serious injury, but you will always get banged up a bit.

Warm up.

Never forgo warming up and stretching. Research proves that injury is likelier to happen to cold muscles. Jumping jacks, stationary cycling, walking or running in place for 3 to 5 minutes make good warm ups. Gentle and slow stretching comes next – hold each stretch for half a minute.

Wear defensive pants.

Padded from the hips to the knees, defensive pants also help guard against bruising and other injuries.

Work on bumping.

To improve a bad bump, keep you knees bent. This is the source of power. Concentrate on maintaining stillness and stiffness in your arms. If you move them up and down a lot, you have a lot less control. Always follow through the motions with both body and eyes. Doing this helps you and your teammates stay focused on where the ball is.

Learn how to set.

The next step towards good playing is knowing how to set. To be a good setter, you must have the stamina to get to the ball anywhere on your side of the court at any time.

You only have three hits to get the ball over the net, so be precise! Setting is used to get the ball in a good position for the striker to strike it. If the striker isn't in position when you're setting the ball, it's your job to get the ball over the net.

Improve bad setting technique.

Hands should always be rigid. The ball should never touch your palms, only your fingertips.

Holding your hands in a diamond shape provides a flatter surface for the ball so it can achieve the ideal bounce. When setting, the ball should go straight up and down and have good height.

Know the most potent move.

The final and most important maneuver in volleyball is the strike. This move wins games, steals points and sends your opponent packing – if you get the point. It's a must-know move. Good strikers are tall, for it's their job to send the ball over the net fast and hard enough to prevent the opponents from returning it. When done correctly, a striker sends the ball over the net directly in the center without missing a beat.

Watch out for the opponent's blockers.

Strikers have to watch out for the other team's blockers. They also should watch out for weak defensive positions on the other team to make their strikes most effective. If you competitor has a good defense, a soft or slanted strike can catch them off guard.

Learn how to strike properly.

Striking the ball forcefully can make or break you. Don't, by any means, strike the ball out of bounds. Of vital importance is trajectory. The goal is to hit the ball over and down so it stays in play. Maintain your legs, for they provide you with the vertical lift necessary to jump up and strike properly. A ref might penalize you for flat-handed strikes, so it's best to work with the power fist.

Take your game to the beach.

If setting the ball is one of the skills you're worst at when playing, and you always seem to be slapping at the ball and it wouldn't go where you wanted, playing two-on-two beach volleyball will really help you improve your game. Opponents will immediately notice if you set poorly, so they'll serve the ball to your teammate, forcing you to set each time. The pressure gets turned on, but it's a trial by fire that really helps you develop your technique. This applies in other situations, like not being a good hitter or passer. Beach volleyball forces you to become a well-rounded player, and it's a perfect way to improve the skills you need to be successful.

Do your research.

Volleyball is a sport geared towards excellent technique. Players with good techniques will nearly always beat better athletes who have poor technique. When learning the game, it helps to have gifted coaches who drill good techniques into their players. A coach or another player who can teach you the proper mechanics is invaluable. If that's not possible, research good volleyball technique on your own over the Internet or elsewhere.

Play as much as you can.

Like anything, the more you work at it, the better you get. Play any chance you get. From beach volleyball tournaments or indoor league play to pickup games with friends, take advantage of every opportunity to play. You can even play pepper with two or three friends during breaks. Continue to pass-set-hit and then dig-set-hit the ball for as long as everyone can keep the ball flying. Your muscular memory will stay sharp and benefit from the repetition the more you play.

Get in shape.

Gaining an edge in competitive volleyball involves more than know-how and performing endless drills. A good way to elevate your game is strength training. A personal trainer may not have any knowledge of the muscle groups you should focus on, which could end up diminishing your game (such as tricep overdevelopment). Check out some of the ways to train and condition specifically for volleyball: Train with an experienced player, hunt down an amateur team and approach one of the players, or post a Craigslist ad and look for local club teams by doing a Google search.

Sign up for a camp.

Certain volleyball camps provide one-on-one training sessions to focus on improving specific areas. Camps may be administered by local colleges, club teams or sports and recreation centers.

Improve your vertical leap.

To improve your vertical leap, purchase shoes made expressly to build your calve muscles.

Look to other sports for certain exercises.

While drilling or playing games, pay attention to the parts of your body you're using and learn the tips and drills for that activity. If you want to improve your quickness on the spike, consider a track & field or football exercise. Rowing or baseball pitching can help you spike the ball harder.

The court is divided with a net, not a wall.

A common phrase used by coaches is, "It's a net, not a wall." The fact that you can see through it can give you an advantage. This may sound simple, but many players wait too long to react to the movement of the ball. Keep your eyes focused through the net, watch the play develop and give yourself more time to react to the play.

23

Serve up more aces.

Being on the lookout for a frustrated, upset, tired or injured player is another way to score additional aces. Should you notice any of those things, tell the server. Such an opponent doesn't really have their head in the game, so send the ball their way and see how they react.

Use bleachers for running drills.

A great way to improve your leaping ability and your quickness is to use bleachers for running drills. You can accomplish this on large or small sets of bleachers. Beginners should start on a small set, running up and down three times. Intermediate players should attempt to complete a large set (15 to 20 rows) at least three times. Experienced players must work with large bleachers with 20+ rows and skip every other step. Take a 30-second break between each set.

Practice good defensive hand position.

Learning good hand position is necessary once you know where to position yourself on the court and how to hold the right defensive stance. A split second can be the difference between a dig and a kill, so good hand technique is vital. Palms should face up as soon as the hitter contacts the volleyball. Should the ball zoom through the block, your hands will be up and ready to pop it up. This may seem trivial, but it's supremely important in the course of a game.

Want to learn all these tips while actually doing them?

Visit
www.ArmChairGuides.com/PlayingVolleyball

Sign up and download
your AUDIO COPY
of **Playing Volleyball: An Arm Chair Guide Full of 100 Tips
to Getting Better at Volleyball**
for FREE.

Need to multitask?
Need to relax your strained eyes after work?
Need to do your laundry?

Pick up some valuable advice to get you started and
integrate it into your lifestyle. Since the tips are being
read aloud, you'll no longer have a reason not to start
playing volleyball.

Stay focused on the competition.

I learned this tip on how to focus a team on the competition from a professional Italian squad: during pre-game stretching exercises, don't line the team up in a circle to face each other. Rather, have them face their opponents while they warm up. In this way, they'll focus and familiarize themselves with their competitors. It may even serve as an intimidation factor.

Jump serve the same way every time.

Few coaches teach players proper jump serve techniques. Jump serving should be the same way every time. When spiking, there are many variables to consider before and during the attack, but a proper jump serve has a limited number of variables.

It's OK to practice the variables when learning the technique, but only in the beginning. Explore the approach, toss, jump and arm swing, but once you feel comfortable, settle on a routine.

After you gain the general feel and technique of the jump serve, the contact should be identical each time. Probably the most important aspect is the contact point. No matter what else is happening, maintaining the same point of contact each time leads to success.

Improve defensive reaction time

Take a ball and stand about 5 to 10 feet from a wall. Toss the ball into the air then spike it hard against the wall to launch it back at you. Practice digging or deflecting the ball into the air or at a target you've marked on the wall.

Once you get the hang of it, hit the ball harder or move a step closer to the wall, and practice deflecting the ball towards different areas with a variety of body parts.

29

Use tennis ball to enhance your spiking skills.

Almost every kid has thrown a baseball or softball, so the body and mind are attuned to this technique. Simply toss a tennis ball against the wall. This shows that the similarities between spiking a volleyball and the throwing motion are in the arm swing and snap of the wrist. It takes the fear out of the learning process because you are familiar with it. You will begin to gain a feeling for the spiking motion by tossing the smaller ball and practicing with it. Then move to the net and stand still, snapping the ball over the net. Next, jump in place while tossing the ball over.

Be consistent when it comes to serving.

Good serves can account for up to 40% of your team's offense. There are numerous types of serves, but they share one thing: the server must be consistent. Develop a routine early in your career, find something that works and stick to it. Routines may involve looking down while you bounce the ball, gathering your focus then looking up, breathing and breaking into the serve. The importance of a good routine should never be underestimated. Perform it exactly the same no matter if it's the game's first serve or a championship match point. Each time is critical. Stick to your routine.

Get your serve to go where you want.

When serving, try pointing your toes, knees, hips and shoulders precisely where you want to send the ball. Give it a go!

Try the wrist snap technique.

Try this wrist snap technique for spikes. Get a kneepad and progress through the approach and into the full arm swing. Toss the pad over the net at the height of your jump, trying to get it as close as possible to the 10' mark. With this drill, the wrist snapping motion at the end of a spike is learned.

Get involved in every play.

The rulers of the net are the middle blockers. Relentlessly aggressive on both offense and defense, they are the warriors of your team and always in motion.

An effective CF (center front) loves working hard and involving him or herself in every play. If you played basketball, you'd be the shot blocker. Dominating the net and making it your own is your task as well as causing opposing hitters to over think, adjust their hits and messing up their game.

34

Block head to head.

For middle blockers, you block head to head, but the angle shot is the easiest and most common hit, especially at lower levels of play. You'll want to stop the angle, forcing your opponent to do other things. If there is nothing else they can do, they'll stop hitting. At this point, you own them, and they're no longer useful to their team.

Look where the setter is.

When blocking during the quickset, identify the position of the setter. Is he or she too far back to be effective? Wait back and anticipate a regular set or an outside shot if so.

Get your hands around the ball when blocking.

When blocking, smother the ball. Try to completely wrap your hands around the ball, pushing it down as you do. This makes it impossible for the ball to go anywhere else but down.

Don't go up to block when the opponent is setting.

It doesn't help to block when they are setting unless your opponent runs a 5-1 offense. If you go up with the setter, precious time is lost that you could otherwise use to get where his or her set is going.

Wait.

If you're blocking a back row attack, wait an additional half second. Be sure you stand a good chance to get to the ball, for your position could impair your teammates' vision as they get ready to dig.

39

Mirror your opponent.

Go one on one with the opposing CF (center front) when blocking. It's similar to man-on-man defense in basketball. When he goes up, so do you. When she moves towards a slide to hit, you must move too. Always mirror the opposing CF unless you're certain she'll be out of the play.

Improve your passing technique.

An effective, inexpensive way to get better at passing simply involves using a one-gallon milk jug. The passer stands above the jug, which is set on the floor, with feet positioned a bit wider than the shoulders and the jug a bit in front. Next, the passer bends the knees while keeping his back straight and eyes forward, and with locked arms, he continues until he touches the jug's handle with his forefingers. With his two fingers, he will pick up the jug, rise up with the knees and, keeping the back straight and eyes forward, place the jug right between his legs. This helps you to never to bend at the waist which diminishes the ability to keep an eye on where the ball is going. This will condition the body to keep a good stance when passing and do away with bad habits that find their way into a player's technique.

41

Touch the ball with only the pads of your fingers when setting.

Since most players are familiar with a deck of cards, they will know what a spade is. A technique taught to beginners is to make a spade with the hands by touching the index fingers and thumbs together. Look up at the space and keep its shape in your mind. Another way to think of it is a "view finder". This kind of visual description helps you learn how to set.

42

Learn by letting the ball fall through.

Balance the ball on your forehead then toss it up and let it fall and hit you smack in the center of your forehead. If you're in the proper position, this drill will reinforce the knowledge of exactly where the ball should hit when setting.

Increase your outside hitting percentage.

You can improve your hitting percentage by forcing the opposing blocker to play you honest. It's simple but infrequently used. To accomplish it, always, without fail, hit your first ball down the line. Simple, right? Blockers are taught to guard the angle until their opponent goes down the line. 90% of hits are at the angle, so hitting your first hit down the line sends a strong message to your opponent. Now they have to play you straight in order to guard the line, and this opens up the angle once again. Try hitting your second shot down the line too. Why? An opposing might assume your first shot was an accident. Because of this, they'll instruct their blockers to guard the angle still until you hit the line, for real this time. You'll get away with another line shot. If they refuse to adjust, hit the line on every shot, and watch your percentage skyrocket.

Try "the death march".

Regardless of your workout method, some coaches insist on "the death march" near the end. It works like this:

Once your regular workout is finished, look for something to jump up to and touch like a backboard.

Stand below the target, and with feet gathered as if you're blocking, jump up and touch it. Once back down, gather again and repeat. Continually repeat the drill until you fail to touch the target three times running. Despite its grueling nature, it pays off big, resulting in a higher jump and increased endurance. (There's a reason they call it the death march).

45

Work both legs together.

Try this exercise on for size: the bunny hop. With feet shoulder width apart, squat and rotate both arms back as if you're performing a full arm swing. While bringing your arms forward, leap ahead as far as you can reach. Land and repeat the process. Move from one end of the gym to the other, rest for a bit and do it again.

You work both legs together which helps, especially for blockers. Being able to jump higher always helps regardless of your position.

No plyometric boxes?

You can always do hopping drills using the bleachers. First, put your hands either on your hips or behind your head. Jump two feet up and onto the first step on the bleachers. Keep doing this for ten reps, with the time spent on the floor as brief as you can. Take a one-minute breather then repeat three times.

Land properly.

Ask any airline pilot: the landing is as important as the takeoff. Every time you land, do so on the balls of the feet. Very briefly, let your full foot come into contact with the floor before springing up again. As with the bleacher hops, the time on the ground should be brief.

Try some plyometric exercises.

A plyometric exercise described in the book *Jumping Into Plyometrics* involves using a multiple-box routine.

Organize a row of three or four boxes of equal height. While squatting, place the hands on hips or behind the head. Spring onto the first box then jump right back down. Spring onto the second box then back down, and repeat for each box. Turn and go back to the starting spot. Do this several times while resting momentarily between sets.

Do jumping exercises.

Try these three jumping exercises to improve vertical height. 30-meter, one-leg hops: starting at the end line, use only the left leg and hop to the center line. Sprint back and repeat, using the right leg this time. Do 5 reps. 30-meter bounds: Bound off the left foot then right, alternately, moving to the center line and sprint back. Do 5 reps. 30-meter approach jumps: Perform a two-step approach to the center line that includes a big leap and full arm swing like you're spiking and sprint back. Do 5 reps.

Introduce two-foot ankle hops

Try this workout: With feet shoulder width apart, keep your body straight. With only the ankles, hop in place continuously. With each jump, extend your ankles to their maximum range. Go for one minute, rest for a minute then go again. Do three sets.

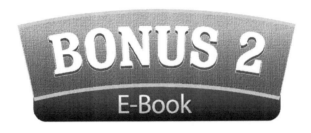

BONUS 2

E-Book

Bring these tips anywhere you go—
on the bus, train or while standing in line!

Head to
www.ArmChairGuides.com/PlayingVolleyball

Sign up and grab
the **Playing Volleyball: An Arm Chair Guide Full of 100 Tips
to Getting Better at Volleyball**
E-BOOK BUNDLE (in PDF, ePub and Mobi) for FREE.

Do you want to read your Arm Chair Guides book on your
device? Do you want to adjust the font size and still be
able to add notes and bookmarks or highlight the text?

Download the free e-book bundle, which comes in 3
popular formats, and view them using your favorite
reader. Learn some valuable tips to prepare for the game
anytime, anywhere.

Jump rope.

Here are a couple rope jumping exercises. First week: On two legs, jump 25 times followed by a minute rest, then jump 50 times. Do 2 reps.

Second through eighth week: On one leg, jump 25 times and work up to 50 during course of season. Do two reps on each leg.

Bound.

An exercise to isolate each leg is called bounding. Bound forward on one leg while landing on the other. Right when landing, bound forward as far as you can off the other leg. It's like skipping, but it's more like "power skipping", as you put total effort into each bound. Do this exercise a couple of times weekly.

Limit your workout in the beginning.

It is recommended that you limit your workout to 20 to 30 minutes in the beginning. Begin with a warm up, light jog, stretching, large arm swings and lateral movements for half the time, then move onto the specialty drills. Follow this with a period of cool down.

Work some jumps into your routine.

Obtain some small orange cones at a sports store, and implement them easily into your routine. Begin with feet shoulder width apart. With bent knees, jump over the cone. Quickly turn and jump back again. Go for one minute, rest for a minute and repeat for three sets. Or set up a row of cones, jump each of them, turn and jump back.

Run sprints.

It is recommended that you do sprints rather than laps while doing your plyometric routine. Volleyball doesn't require long distance jogs, so you want to increase quickness and vertical height.

Watch the hitter.

A good tip to remember while defending is to watch the hitter, looking for the ball behind their head when chasing down a line or a deep shot. There's no need to guess where the ball will go if you watch the hitter.

Find the right jump serve method for you.

Individual tips on rhythm and toss vary from person to person. If you're a quick hitter, you might prefer a quick toss to a high toss. There is no one right way to do things, and since everyone is different, find the best method that suits your jump serve style.

Build up your confidence.

One tip that will improve your game no matter your style is to remember that if you lack confidence, your game will suffer. As in life, it's the little things that tend to be the difference makers. Through experience, you'll develop more and more confidence. Playing whenever you can is the best way to build your skills and your confidence level.

Stick with your technique.

In tight, game-time situations, stick with your technique. At all times, keep things simple and adhere to the fundamentals. It's the key to success because it keeps you from focusing on outside influences.

Watch out for negative movement.

This means to be wary of extra or unnecessary action. To give you an example, when passing, imagine all the space below your platform to be negative space into which you cannot dip. If you do this always, you will develop good habits.

Use soft hands.

Your hands should be above your head with slightly cocked wrists as the ball approaches. As it comes into contact with your hands, cushion the ball by flexing then straightening your wrists in a fast motion. To move the ball to the chosen hitter, use both hands in an equal manner.

There is a fine line between using soft hands to cushion the ball and getting penalized for illegally holding the ball for a split second too long. You'll appear to carry the ball if your wrists give too much, you'll be penalized, and your opponent will score a point.

Have strong hands.

Hands shouldn't be too stiff, though. You'll never control the ball properly without some give in your wrists. With a forearm pass, you channel the ball's momentum toward a target when you let it bounce off of your arms. By contrast, setting requires you to adjust the ball's path as it goes up from your hands.

When it comes the setter's way, the ball is actually moving towards the net. A good set has the ball moving parallel with the net. If your hands don't provide a soft cushion without holding too long, you can't alter the ball's path and set it accurately.

Thumbs to your eyes.

This is not to say that you actually poke your eyes with your thumbs. The idea is, as you receive the ball, your thumbs should be positioned right above your eyes.

Flex your wrists slightly and round your fingers to achieve this position. Your thumbs should be directed toward your face; they'll be in the way of the ball if they're not pulled back, and they could get jammed.

Remember to cushion the ball without carrying it, and to do this you need properly shaped hands. To get them into their spherical shape, pull the thumbs toward your eyes.

You will achieve a more consistent set when you make sure your thumbs are not pointing towards your forehead or mouth.

Learn from other sports.

To learn accurate ball position when setting, volleyball players can learn from soccer players even though they only use their feet. To be more specific, it has to do with heading the ball.

With accurate footwork and the proper position, when the ball heads towards you in preparation for setting, it should be approaching your forehead. The ball should hit your forehead, not your mouth or crown, if you were to move your hands away at the last second. But don't actually let the ball hit your face.

In this way, you'll take full advantage of your arm power, wrists and muscles in your legs. Keeping a good position every time lets you limit the amount of time the ball is in your hands, so you're less likely to be penalized.

Determine the height, amount of bend and force.

Consider how high you toss the ball, how much you bend your elbow, and how hard your hit is when serving. You'll need to practice each of these things separately to develop a good routine. Your serve with be flat or have a high trajectory depending on how you strike the ball. You'll be able to alter your serve as you please once you know and understand the different volleyball techniques. Watch a live demonstration of a game of volleyball to see how to serve effectively.

To serve, toss the ball above your serving shoulder, strike it directly in the middle with the palm of your hand and follow through the full swing while keeping your elbow above the level of your head.

Anticipate ball direction when setting.

This refers to the move where you set the ball up in such a way that it's easy for a teammate to slam the ball into your competitor's side of the court. Setters must anticipate ball direction, and they have to know that they will get the right opportunity to set the ball accurately.

Improve your passing skill.

Accuracy and precision are important when passing because it comes before setting. A passer should not be heavy handed, and their passes should always let the setter achieve good ball direction with their set. A passer must have good movement and take soft, slow steps.

It's up to the fingers to properly pass the ball, while the passer relies on the hips to move. Verbal communication with the setter is very important.

Footwork is key.

The player's footwork is instrumental in techniques that pertain to advanced hitting and ball-attacking moves. Accuracy and power behind the shot are the results of good footwork. Expert control of the last two steps before the shot are vital.

How you approach the ball, swing the shoulders and the top spin you give the ball also play important roles in good hitting.

Know which shots to block.

Because it requires great vision, blocking is one of the harder points of volleyball. A blocker has to know which shots to block and which to leave alone. Blockers must decide which move is right, and he has to do it fast.

Footwork is very important as well as the shape of the fingers when blocking. It benefits the entire squad when the members of the team communicate with each other.

Practice proper digging.

When blockers miss and the ball seems to be heading to the ground resulting in a point for the opponents, this is where diggers come in. Requiring great reflexes and agility, any player may have to dig in a game. You have to drop to the ground fast and lift the ball up so a teammate can get it. It takes regular practice to dig effectively.

Have an attack mindset.

Like any competitive team sport, the goal of volleyball is to win. A good serve helps a team's chances. Getting the ball over the net is just one aspect of a serve. Serves can score points for the team, while bad serves assist the other team to score.

You should have an attack mindset when serving. It's possible to score with the serve. Thus, it's the first point of attack. To be successful, be mentally aggressive from the start.

Be aware of your position.

To serve better, notice your position. You shouldn't step on or over the back line when serving. You will not improve your serve by standing as close to the line as possible, and it could cost your team points if you cross it. With feet planted firmly, stand upright: one foot back (matching serving hand) and one foot forward (opposite serving hand). Keeping good posture, your movement becomes the focus.

Keep the ball in the same place each serve.

Get good at tossing the ball up. With the ball held in front of you (in non-hitting hand), throw it up about two feet above your head at a distance of one foot in front of your body. You need to toss it up identically each time. Doing so will help the ball clear the net and improve your precision. Your serve will be weak or unpredictable if you have to adjust your whole body because you throw the ball up in a different manner each time.

Keep your arm raised high when serving.

A common mistake of volleyball players is not raising the arm high enough. Raise your arm so that your elbow is higher than ear level to ensure the ball gets over the net.

75

Keep your target in front of you.

Point your body toward where you intend on serving the ball. It could be a certain player or an area on the court, but when you line up in a single direction, it allows you to put all of your focus on the ball. When practicing, mark distinct areas on the opposing court and practice landing the ball in each one.

BONUS 3

Weekly Tips for 1 Year

Get the Tip of the Week delivered straight to your inbox!

Head to
www.ArmChairGuides.com/PlayingVolleyball

Sign up
for the **Playing Volleyball: An Arm Chair Guide Full of 100 Tips to Getting Better at Volleyball**
NEWSLETTER.

Join the Arm Chair Guides Newsletter and get a quick volleyball tip each week for one whole year.

Smack the ball right in its center spot with an open palm.

If you hit it on one side or the other, the serve is weaker and the ball may spin to one side. If you hit it too low, the back will spin backwards. Side-handed serves or serving with only a partially opened hand leads to unpredictability. Improve the strength, speed and accuracy of your serve by attending to where and just how you hit the volleyball.

Always, always practice!

Continuous practice leads to better serves. Teams engage in hundreds or thousands of training sessions before they ever win a championship. If you want to be a champion, the practice is worth it.

Start with your feet.

For setting, good fundamentals begin with your feet. Foot movement determines how well you perform each technique. Start with your feet shoulder width apart, comfortably so with slightly bent knees. Right-handed players should position their right foot two inches ahead of the left foot. The opposite is true for left-handed players. This leads to better balance when setting on the run.

Focus on the form of the midsection of your body.

Whether you are standing still or moving towards the ball, imagine there is an iron rod glued to your back from your tail bone to the top of your neck. This rod prevents you from bending over at the waist, allowing you only to squat up or down and forcing you to use your footwork to assume the right position. For the set, this is the correct movement and posture – bends your knees and squat underneath the ball then lift your body up and out of the squat while straightening your legs when coming into contact with the ball. (Think of it like having to stand up and meet the ball from a seated position with your hands above your head).

Take note of where your arms are.

With your elbows at a 90-degree angle like when running, your arms should be at your sides. Bring your arms up and in front of you when the ball is about two feet above your head. As they come up, bring them together. As your hands reach chest level, bring them together so your thumbs and index fingers can form a diamond shape.

Be aware of your hand position.

The palms of both hands should face the sky to form the correct hand position when setting. They should be relaxed and open in order to fit perfectly around the ball as it makes contact. The forefingers and thumbs should barely touch and form a broken triangle or diamond shape which you hold directly above your forehead.

Work on your passing stance.

Good, effective passing involves maintaining an athletic posture, so you are always ready to react and move in an instant.

Stay relaxed yet poised and ready to move. The knees should be flexed comfortably, and your weight should be centered on the balls of the feet.

83

Be quick and aggressive with your footwork when passing.

This will allow you to have time to get in front of the ball. First, step with the foot closest to the ball. Don't let your head bounce when moving. The earlier you arrive to play the ball, the better. When you get there early, you can adjust your foot position.

Read the direction of the ball.

Track the ball as soon as it leaves the server's hand until it reaches your arms if you are a passer. Watch the server's contact and the ball's movement as it reaches your end of the court. Notice if the ball spins or floats so you can read its direction.

Get into the rhythm.

Get in the habit of reacting as soon as you can tell where the ball will end up. If you wait too long, you may struggle to get into the proper passing position.

Keep a high platform.

Platform means the total arm area that comes into contact with the ball when passing. The platform must be at the right angle to pass effectively, or else it can be difficult. As you ready yourself to pass, make your platform parallel with the ground. You will not be able to follow through towards the target if your platform isn't up and ready.

Follow through.

Passing methods differ from coach to coach. It doesn't matter if it involves specific footwork or another thing that needs to be done. I've played for years and noticed numerous styles, but there is one thing successful passing techniques have in common. That one thing is following through towards your target. Wherever you are on the court, your back leg should always move in the direction the ball moves. For instance, if passing with your right foot forward, use your left foot to follow through. The same is true for all positions when passing.

Use your legs – don't swing.

Here's another commonly used technique. If players pass only using their arms, they tend to swing. Even though it works sometimes, it isn't the best method. A ball coming at you hard shouldn't be swung at, otherwise off it will go. Instead of swinging your arms, keep your platform up and steady and meet the ball by adjusting the position of your legs.

89

Watch as the ball makes contact with platform.

With this tip, beginners gain a better understanding of the types of errors that cause errant passes. Keep your eyes on the ball as you raise your platform in preparation to pass. As you make contact with the ball, watch it continuously until it reaches the target. Consistency achieved by repetition is the secret to great passing, as well as other aspects of the game. Keep these tips in mind each time you make a pass and see how you improve.

Study your movements on video.

Analyzing your hitting form helps you improve. Have someone record your hits onto video. Have them film from the front, the back and side to see your hitting arm from all directions. Slow motion reveals small details. Check your form and your timing. Notice your position and whether your body bends in the air each time you go up to hit the ball. Notice the direction in which you jump. Notice how high you are when hitting the ball. Develop an understanding of the things you tend to do. Where do your strengths lie? In this way, you can improve any weak aspects of your game. Have a coach or knowledgeable player help you identify areas that need improvement.

Take a quick look at the defenders' positions.

A good hitter can pick out a weak point in the defense and know where to place the ball exactly where the defenders are not. To do this, you have to be able to use your peripheral vision.

Notice how much of the court you can see, both what you look directly at and how much you see out of the corner of your eye. Are any open spots visible? Where should you send the ball to make a point? Do you notice any vulnerability in a blocker? It's important to develop good peripheral vision on the court and away from it. Keep your eyes trained on a point and practice using your peripheral vision to make contact with your targets.

Develop your ability to pick up the block and hit it properly.

There is more to being a good hitter than sending the ball down. A good hitter is smart. A good hitter scores more points by tooling the block. In tight sets where your team is forced into a duel, the team that pushes the ball last has the last laugh.

Increase your strength.

Lifting weights will help you hit the ball harder. By doing so, you will avoid injury by strengthening your bones. You will become a better hitter by developing your jumping ability and the muscles in your gut, back and shoulders. A hitter uses nearly every muscle in his body, but due to the repetition, the shoulders are the most vulnerable to injury.

Stabilize your shoulders by using the rowing machine and reverse fly. Sit-ups help to strengthen your core. To get you up in the air, you use your glutes, hams, quads and calf muscles. Leg presses, leg extensions, leg curls and calf raises build those muscles. Also beneficial are lunges.

Work with your setter when hitting.

In this game, you always have to communicate. Always let you setter know any adjustments you've made after analyzing your form and improving it. Maybe she can help out. There are things she can do to augment your new approach. Maybe it's a higher set or a faster set that's needed. By working one-on-one with the setter, you'll both be clearer about the best way to achieve a better all-around game.

Be aggressive during an overpass.

Tight, overset passes can be trouble. Back-row setters can't do much more than fake or back off and prepare to dig out a hit. With tight passes, the front-row setter should be aggressive and prepared to joust.

Even though the blocker is higher up than you, the player with lower hand position tends to win, so this can be to your advantage when jousting. This position lets you push the ball down under the hands and arms of the blocker, so she is neutralized.

End with a follow-through.

Finishing the block is a trait of the best blockers. Like what a baseball player does when hitting or pitching, a blocker follows through. The ball hitting your hands is not the end of the block. Only when the ball hits the floor is the block over. Giving a final push with your arms, wrists and hands off the block is the most effective way to push the ball to the floor. You should feel the follow through motion even if you miss the block and the ball passes through.

Swipe to surprise a jouster.

Whenever you manage to successfully joust the ball (and maybe even your opponent) to the floor, you've done good. That's a challenge most blockers can't resist, but there are other ways to get the better of your opponent.

The expectation is you will always try to push the ball into the attacker's hands. Try surprising him next time by swiping the ball to one side. In so doing, the ball is directed to the side of the court and away from his hands. You want to swipe as hard as you can and still stay in control and not touch the net.

Square up if you can't make it there.

It's the middle blocker's job to react quickly and always jump. They are prone to misreading plays and come in late when an outside set is going down. Try this to make up ground when the occasional late block happens.

Stay square to the net if you're late to the outside, but you can still reach a little. You keep your hips, shoulders, arms and hands parallel with the plane of the net when staying square. Don't turn towards the hitter. Problems will arise if you do. The ball could deflect out of bounds if you touch it. Secondly, holes open up in your block. If you're reaching properly, your wall will still be up and effective.

Track the ball.

When blocking, never close your eyes or drop your head. These can be hard habits to break despite the practice you put in. Try keeping your eye on the ball when attacking it. You can break these bad habits by watching the hitter as he contacts the ball.

Watching the ball all the time lets you capitalize on an opponent's weak link. Do this and you might be able to extend your arm and successfully swat the ball.

Always go for the ball on top of the net.

As a back-row setter, the attacking rule states you can't try to set a ball that breaks the plane of the net when an opposing blocker touches it, or you will be whistled for a penalty. As a blocker, the play continues if you let the setter set the ball. Your team will get the side out or point if you so much as touch the ball.

Block a ball set by the front-row setter who attempts the same type of set. Basically, you never want the setter to get off a set when the ball is at the top of the net. It's up to you to decide if the ball has broken the plane of the net because if not, you'll be penalized for blocking an attempt at second contact that is totally legal.

Conclusion

Volleyball is a fun, active sport enjoyed throughout the world. There is no costly equipment to buy, and the game can be learned quickly. You can play inside a gym or outside in a park, backyard or on a beach. Like many things, volleyball is easy to pick up, but it takes a lot of practice to develop real skill at it. If you have the desire to get good at volleyball, spend time working on your techniques, get into good workout habits and play as much as you can!